velvet dragonflies

velvet dragonflies

BILLY CHAPATA

Andrews McMeel
PUBLISHING®

flight.

the path back to yourself will be unique.

it won't be a linear journey filled with straightforward results and outcomes, it won't be a **smooth** sail with consistently calm waves and peaceful winds, it won't be a transparent trail with clear signs and direction—it will be incomparable.

it will have a variety of experiences that will leave you feeling a multitude of things at different times;

sometimes, you will experience much that will leave you heavy.

sometimes, you will experience much that will leave you **lighter**.

other times, your experiences will serve no other purpose than helping you grow **wings** so you can return back home, to you.

time may have hardened your heart, but you are deserving of nothing but **softness**; time may have roughened your spirit, but you are deserving of nothing but **gentleness**; time may have tainted the opinion you have of yourself, but you are deserving of nothing but **forgiveness.** i hope, eventually, these words open you to the realization that you are deserving of all those things and much more.

contents

viscose.

silly me,

i was the right person for me all along.

hello, i know i've forgotten about you recently. how nice it is to meet you again. it feels nice, doesn't it? to feel so familiar yet so transformed. i guess time has a way of making you realize what is more important, and now i realize that it was always you.

—a letter to my self

(better late than never)

i'm learning to love my own language again.

i'm learning to pronounce it loud even
when they don't understand me.

i'm learning to give it a voice even if its accent is unfamiliar.

i'm learning to stop spelling it out to the wrong ears.

i'm learning to love my own language again.

i hope

you learn to heal the parts of you that feel the need to constantly apologize for things that you are not responsible for in fear that they may leave or get upset if you don't take ownership of the guilt they are trying to place on you. i hope you realize that you are not a place mat for people's fears and insecurities.

losing battles.

how many connections have you fought for,
knowing deep down that you would be better off without them?
how many connections have you fought for,
because the thought of being alone scares you?
how many connections do you still fight for,
when you really should be **letting go**?

(there are greater things waiting for you beyond everything that once gave you comfort)

some doors must remain closed. not because you won't be able
to handle the truth behind them, but because your narrative has
outgrown all the trauma that those old things may have brought you.
not everything that was once for you, is still for you.

misplaced energy.

it's a much deeper kind of self-sabotage
when you continuously search for people,
when you still haven't found yourself.

spacious revolutions.

be there for you, more.
be more for you, often.
there is love that you've relinquished,
that you should've been pouring back into you all along.
there is energy that you've exerted
on people and situations that don't deserve your time.
make more room for you.

(love yourself so deeply that if anyone were to ever leave, love for yourself would still remain)

people come, and call it love.
people stay, and call it love.
people go, and call it love.
but this is why you must become love,
so that regardless of what they
do or do not do, you still remain **full**.

(it goes both ways)

just as easily as you can outgrow people,
people can easily outgrow you too.
no two paths are the same, no two journeys are identical,
and people are allowed to become who they are
without you attaching bitterness or sadness to their evolution.

that thing that you're holding on to so tightly;

let it go and see if it comes back. give it a chance to show you if it's real.

(my love language is not one that everyone can speak or one that everyone has spoken)

you can't love me the same way you loved old lovers.
i'm a different kind of lover.

<u>self-acceptance.</u>

i'm past the stage of fighting to be understood,
and fully invested in the idea of understanding
myself better than anyone else ever could.

eventually,

you will get tired of feeling sorry for people who don't want to help themselves, and when that day comes, you will realize that you are not responsible for anyone's healing but your own.

(the loss of a connection can be one of the most beautiful things to ever happen to you. give the space that comes with loss the freedom to manifest into something fruitful for you)

the friendships that no longer exist
birthed the friendship i should've
had with myself all along.
sometimes people need to move
out of your path so you can
see yourself again.

viscose.

if it doesn't give me peace,
it will give me **growth**.

(your healing never truly begins until you are completely honest and transparent with yourself. when you take your wounds out on a date and leave your ego at home. when you take responsibility for your healing and remove the ownership from anyone else's hands. your healing truly begins when you stop projecting and internalizing, and start reflecting and being more vulnerable about your pain)

i found healing
when i told ego to lower its voice and sit in the corner
while i asked my wounds important questions.

viscose.

__authentic bonds.__

there is no connection more powerful
than two people bringing their individualities
to the table with no intention
of diluting each other's essence but instead,
celebrating what makes each other unique.

(every part of you is deserving of love regardless of how broken you think it is)

your healing will take time. it will require patience and softness. but never let the frustration of how long it's taking poison your spirit. there are parts of you that haven't healed fully that still deserve love.

light transformations.

who you used to be, isn't who you are now.
who you used to be, isn't who you're required to be.
you don't have to carry your past in your wallet
if it's no longer what you identify with.
you are allowed to empty your pockets
to feel **lighter** from everything that weighs you down.

**expensive housing.**

nostalgia will keep you renting space in toxic places
and swimming in muddy waters if you allow it to. your
peace of mind is more valuable than old memories and
your growth has no room to operate on sympathy.

ego will keep you repeating the same mistakes because you feel like
the lesson being taught is one that doesn't apply to you, or one that
doesn't feed into your spirit. manage your ego enough to gain the
clarity to see what is in front of you and to see what needs to change.

fear will keep you in cycles that seem never-ending, while
doubt lurks in the background playing games with your
soul. drown your worries and concerns in honesty and
light, so you can finally meet with your future.

viscose.

(there are depths that exist within you that can't be reached by everyone. there is language that exists within you that won't be understood by everyone. there is energy that exists within you that can't be matched by everyone, but you are not required to adjust yourself to those that are not at your level)

never shallow your intellectualism just to make people who can't swim in your mind more comfortable. your waves of energy may be too intense for some, or too confusing for others, but your waves are not meant for everyone to float in.

(gentle nudges from the universe)

some energy isn't worth revisiting.
some energy isn't worth exploring.
some energy isn't worth holding onto.
some energy is just a reminder that you
don't have to rely outward to feel **whole**.

viscose.

forgive yourself

for all the times you blamed yourself for letting something good slip away.
if it was for you, then it would've stayed,
if it wasn't, then it only made room for something better.

understand

that some people are only able to handle older versions of you. they will turn away from who you are currently because they don't know what growth looks like. you are not required to reprise older roles you once assumed to make other people comfortable.

viscose.

(some lessons you only learn when you finally tell ego to lower its voice)

there is nothing wrong with waiting for the answers to find you.
sometimes rushing for clarity can lead you further
from the truth and closer to unhappiness.
just remember, when the answers knock on your door and find you,
open your mind, **quiet your ego,** and listen.

you're what i needed, but not what i need anymore.

it feels rough on the tongue to say, but i mean this in the gentlest of ways. it might feel malicious, but believe me when i say my words are wrapped in gratitude. hindsight has a way of taking the blindfolds off and revealing truth. hindsight has a way of washing off all the sugar that's stuck on lies. hindsight has a way of exposing what's not for you and disclosing what's meant to stay. we may have come into each other's space at a time when comfort eluded us and found peace in each other. we may have come into each other's space at a time when we needed direction and drew maps to each other's soul. we may have come into each other's space at a time when life had us on edge and gave each other rope. but times change, situations change, people change, and we are no different. i'm thankful for everything you have ever done, but i'm even more thankful to you for helping me become the person i needed to be. the universe never aligns two paths together for no reason, and even though it was temporary, the lessons i took from our connection are written in permanent ink. i'm learning that some connections have expiration dates, and that's okay. i'm learning that some people are meant to play supporting roles in your life instead of starring ones, and that's okay. i'm learning that sometimes you need to move to where there is more growth, and that's okay. i'm learning that you may have been what i needed, but you're not what i need anymore, and that's okay.

higher discernment.

i used to be drawn to pain like moths are to flames,
only now i won't burn myself for pain that doesn't belong to me.
a healer and a sacrificial lamb are two very different things,
and i'm learning to choose my roles more wisely.

warm noise.

my love is loud,
but it could never silence your insecurities.
my love is loud,
but it could never drown out your doubt.
my love is loud,
but the love you have for yourself
should be louder than the love i have for you.

viscose.

remember:

it is not your duty to wake up anyone that
has been sleeping on your magic.

to whom this may concern: don't be so hard on your older self. try not to judge how you moved or lacked the courage to. you wouldn't be who you are or who you are becoming without them. feed yourself with compassion instead of spoonfuls of regret.

to whom this may concern: give yourself the freedom to make mistakes. give yourself the space to fail. give yourself the room to re-create yourself as many times as you need while using the pieces you've gathered from your missed steps to create a stronger you.

to whom this may concern: sometimes not knowing where to turn is a sign in itself. sometimes feeling lost is not an indication of where you'll always be. sometimes the most movement you can make is in accepting that where you are currently is exactly where you need to be.

viscose.

what looks like peace and happiness on the outside
is actually sleepless nights and long days on the inside.

—*shadow work*

reminder:

you will inspire many who will have absolutely no desire or intention of acknowledging that you ever did. what isn't genuine or from the source always exposes itself eventually—**authenticity can never be replicated.**

viscose.

(secrets about me)

i like my space,
and if you're unable to understand that,
then you're already taking up too much.

spiritual releases.

some love i let go, because i wasn't ready.
some love i let go, because i was naive.
some love i let go, because i didn't understand what love is.
some love i let go, because they let me go.
some love i let go, to prove to myself that i am all i ever needed.

viscose.

(connections run their course for many reasons, but sometimes those reasons are to aid in your emancipation)

good people don't always end up together.
not because two good people can't coexist within a connection,
but because sometimes your **purpose runs much
deeper** than who you are as individuals.

attentive.

when you find love that listens,
you will never need to shout to be heard.
when you find love that listens,
you will never need to over-explain yourself to be felt.
when you find love that listens,
you will never need to look for ears that understand.

viscose.

how many more times

are you going to apologize for being you
instead of just accepting that not everyone can handle
the version of yourself that you are currently?

(lay your weapons down, love)

you've dissected yourself in the mirror too many times for lovers that see you as nothing more than food for their ego, and eventually, i hope you find love that takes the weapons out of your hands and reassures you that you don't have to go to war with yourself for anyone.

viscose.

**muse.**

a woman who is art cannot be replicated.
you cannot trace an image of her soul and make it your own.
she runs deeper than the eye—**she's a feeling**.

(don't continue to suffer in silence)

delayed conversations are poison to a heart that has much to say.

if it frees you, give it a voice.

if it frees you, don't let it turn into unhealed resentment.

gateways.

the longer you go without holding them accountable, the longer they will continue to diminish your worth. how you treat yourself will always set the precedent for how they treat you.

a lover that pours fuel into your passions instead of water.

a lover that sees happiness in your growth and not intimidation.

a lover who injects energy into your dreams when you're running low.

a lover like this.

viscose.

listen:

i'm an easy person to make a home out of,
but my energy is never an invitation to stay.

(how the love for myself makes you feel has nothing to do with me)

some people aren't ready for someone who
is deeply in love with themselves.
they will constantly compete with the energy you treat yourself with
instead of just accepting that your boundaries are a form of self-love.

viscose.

(there is much more out there)

are you tolerating what you think will come good?
or are you settling because you don't feel like you can attract better?
you don't have to prolong pain because
pain is what you're familiar with.

i stayed because i felt like i owed you;

for the times you were present, and for the times that i wasn't. for the times you left your heart on the table, and i left my words standing at the front door. for the times you dove deep to reach me, and i allowed myself to drown. i stayed because my thoughts held me hostage, while guilt stared me down and told me i was wrong for even considering letting go. i stayed because the time and energy we put into our connection is something we could never get back, and what kind of person would i be to let something good go to waste? but did we have something good? or did we just pretend as if we did? if everything was as rosy as we painted it to be, then why did i feel so disconnected from you? why did i feel so disconnected from "us"? but staying because you feel indebted to someone defeats the purpose, doesn't it? how are you repaying the faith someone has in you by staying where you don't want to be? how are you repaying the love someone has for you by overstaying where you've outgrown? how selfish it was of me to keep dangling the possibility of forever in your face. how selfish it was of me to stay in a space where i knew i could never reciprocate fully. how selfish i was to myself for betraying my truth and turning my back on me. i guess sympathy has a way of jading your judgment, and maybe i had been sympathetic for way too long. i stayed because i felt like i owed you, but maybe the only thing that i owed myself was the happiness that you could never give me.

viscose.

(you chose right)

out of all the people you could've fallen in love with,
you chose to fall in love with yourself,
and **there is nothing more romantic**.

(i prefer truth over comfort)

some spaces only feel good
because they don't hold your
toxic traits accountable.
a lack of disagreement
isn't always an indication
of a healthy environment

viscose.

(some people will never be ready, no matter how much they tell you that they love you. putting your life on hold in hopes that their "love" will come to fruition will only poison you slowly)

holding on to potential love for too long in hopes that flowers will grow from the seeds you've planted is dangerous territory to be in. i hope you learn to discern the difference between mature love and love that isn't ready.

understand this;

you don't lose anything by being genuinely happy for someone else. in the same breath, being happy for someone doesn't mean that you have to find space to accommodate them in your life.

soul filters.

your low points always give you insight into your connections.
they unmask the ones who disguise themselves as helping hands
and solidify the presence of the ones with pure intentions.
let your low points sift through your connections.
let your low points filter through your energy.

love for yourself can never arrive too late. you can start your internal revolution today, without beating yourself up for all the times you never loved yourself enough in the past.

you can begin now.

what kind of person would rather hold on to pride than be wrong?

—a person that doesn't value what they have. a person driven carelessly by ego. a person in love with the idea of you.

(things about her)

there's a divine duality about her.
she's full of love,
but she also knows her worth enough
to know not to entertain anything
that diminishes the love she has for herself.
it's either you add to her existence
or you fail to exist to her.

house keys.

i stopped renting out space in my heart when i realized that no one could ever own me regardless of how much they like the idea of me.

i stopped renting out space in my mind when i realized that no one can control me regardless of how my energy makes them feel.

i belong to me always.

**mantra;**

i am flourishing,
with or without your energy,
with or without your opinion,
with or without your acceptance,
with or without your blessing,
with or without your love,
with or without you,
i am flourishing.

viscose.

(it's a beautiful thing for your words to be received gently. it's a beautiful thing to present your concerns without having to worry about your intentions being misconstrued. it's a beautiful thing to show up fully and know that you won't be pushed back into the shadows. it's a beautiful thing to be accepted unconditionally)

you deserve connections that don't require you to walk on eggshells to get a point across.

you deserve connections that don't require you to sacrifice your peace just to protect feelings or egos.

you deserve connections that don't require you to distance your self from yourself.

affirmation:

love that doesn't pick and choose
which parts of you are worthy.
love that doesn't pick and choose
when you are worth showing up for.
love that doesn't pick and choose
if your battles are worth fighting for.
this is love you are worthy of.

(healing is an intimate practice. it requires you to spend time understanding why your wounds hurt. it requires you to exert energy asking your wounds what causes the pain. it requires you to show up for yourself fully, without looking outward for emancipation)

solitude is oxygen to heal. you will fight many battles behind the curtains that no one is aware of. you will encounter internal wars that you must fight alone because only you can grasp the extent of your pain. you will have to spend one-on-one time with your wounds to ascend.

just so you know;

it's no hard feelings.
the love is there,
but the love for myself
is just a little bit stronger.

skin deep.

give people time to learn your love language,
but be honest enough with yourself to know
when your love language isn't for them.
connection runs deeper than laughs and hugs,
compatibility runs deeper than patience and tolerance,
comfort runs deeper than closeness and chemistry.

sometimes,

i look back at certain phases and feel like i may have stayed for too long. but at other times, i look back and feel like i stayed long enough to learn what i needed to. understanding pain is just as therapeutic as letting it go.

viscose.

(nothing personal)

i wish you well,
but from a **distance**.

(your feelings are important)

never abandon your truth trying to polish someone else's. the way you feel is valid and you don't have to change the way you feel just to make other people feel more comfortable about their own truth.

(forgive them both for acting to their level of consciousness)

    forgive your mother for not finding the language to speak up for
what she believes in; forgive your father for not being tender enough
to comprehend her pain. forgive them both, but in the same breath,
thank them for showing you what kind of connections you deserve.

treachery lane.

memories are a dangerous thing to be in love with.
i hope you learn to discern the difference between
the love you have for someone
and the love you have for the moments you spent together.

viscose.

(it feels good now, but does it do anything for you in the long run?)

temporary comfort will not heal your unresolved trauma. you can only rest in fleeting energy for so long before the cracks in your heart that you papered over start to open again. your healing process deserves something thicker than water and glue.

blatant beginnings.

find no shame in starting over.

find no shame in going back to the root and beginning again.

find no shame in rerouting because the path
you took no longer gives you life.

find no shame in admitting that you made mistakes along the way.

find no shame in starting over.

viscose.

healthy divides.

if i said that i love you, i meant it.
if i say that i love myself, i mean it.
so never be surprised if i keep my distance,
with no animosity or resentment attached
to the space between us.
i am entitled to my boundaries
even if they do not make sense to you.

(the opinion you have of yourself outweighs whatever opinions they may have of you)

what you know about yourself is more important than what people think your intentions are. not everyone will choose to see the good in you, but what people think of you has nothing to do with who you are. don't muddy your own water by wiping away dirt that doesn't belong to you.

i hope

you find the strength to walk away from any lover who only chooses to see half of you because they can't handle all of you. you deserve love that appreciates you in your entirety, not just in the parts they find easy to love and in the qualities they find desirable.

(clarity comes in the form of distance too)

sometimes the space between you and an old
connection doesn't need a narrative.

sometimes accepting that you are in two different places in your lives
is all the explanation you need.

you are enough,
even without the clarity you think you need or deserve.

viscose.

i pray,

that you never become so familiar with pain that you reject anything good that tries to find you.

koigu.

new scopes.

i view things differently now,
so if you're still looking at me
from the lens i used yesterday,
you probably won't see me.

koigu.

fresh wounds.

healing is not the complete disappearance of your pain and trauma.
healing is acknowledging that the pain may still exist
but knowing that whatever you've gone
through or whatever you're feeling
doesn't define you.

what kind of love gets intimidated by your internal revolutions and your external accomplishments? what kind of love gets jealous of your growth and scared by your potential? what kind of love walks away when it senses you getting closer to yourself?

—a love you don't need

koigu.

lately,

i've seen you dancing by the fire a lot more recently. by that, i mean that i've seen you flirting with the idea of running back into hands that once burned you. loneliness won't make an old flame burn differently.

(know enough to know better)

looking back, my biggest fear was not being understood.
now, my biggest fear is losing understanding of myself.
so, if you ever come into my life with blurred intentions
and threaten to pull me away from myself,
chances are i'll probably pull myself away from you.

koigu.

(it doesn't always come all at once)

sometimes forgiveness comes in stages.
you will bounce between letting go and holding on
several times before you're ready to move forward.

(there is more to you than what you have to offer other people)

you listen and help them unpack whenever they feel heavy, but where do you put your bags when life is weighing you down? you are more than a lifeboat and an anchor; you don't have to spend your life being an emotional sponge for hands that aren't willing to give you a release.

(my willingness to see the best in you doesn't mean that i will tolerate anything you throw my way)

never confuse my capacity to see the good in people with being unable to see people for who they are. i'll always give you the benefit of the doubt, but once you show me who you are and if it doesn't match up with your intentions, i'll create boundaries to protect my energy.

vulnerability & visibility.

your inner child is still waiting for you to listen to all the
things other people ignored when you were younger.

your inner child is still waiting to be received by arms that
hold your concerns with the same amount of weight.

your inner child is still waiting to be seen, **by you**.

**temporary vibrations.**

some connections grow stale.
not because of any fault of the people within the connection,
but because some connections have expiration dates.
some connections are only meant to serve a purpose
for a short amount of time before you move
into spaces with more growth.
allow them to.

(how much of your suffering do you prolong simply because of non-existent understandings?)

how much of your suffering do you prolong
simply because you can't say "no"?
how much of your suffering do you prolong
simply because you say "yes" too often?

—*boundaries*

good karma.

sometimes you don't attract what you think you deserve;
instead,
you attract a lesson that you're supposed to learn.

(many will tell you that they love you, but few will be able to show you)

love without a language is just a **word**.

(just because you want to help someone doesn't mean that you should. that doesn't make you malicious or inconsiderate, but sometimes people need to unlock healing for themselves. sometimes, constantly pushing them toward a destination isn't what is going to help them get there. sometimes, involving yourself isn't going to lessen the load for them. sometimes, all you can do is support them through their healing while they figure out the answers for themselves. sometimes, they've got to want it more than you want it for them)

one of the biggest lessons you can ever learn is that it is not up to you to awaken someone else's healing. it is not up to you to awaken that dormant volcano of warmth that exists within them in hopes that they erupt love for themselves. they've got to want it more than you do.

bittersweet.

the honeymoon phase is a dangerous space to reminisce on.
love evolves,
the way you love people evolves,
the way they love you evolves.
being stuck on how it was when it tasted sweeter
will only sour your spirit.

koigu.

(secrets about me)

i used to be infatuated with perfection until my
imperfections showed me what love is.

__ascension.__

when love for someone starts jeopardizing
the love you should have for yourself,
then it's never worth it.
love shouldn't hinder you,
it should elevate you.
love should never silence you,
it should give you a voice.
love should never weigh you down,
it should help you **grow wings**.

koigu.

(redirect your energy back home)

empathy becomes expensive
when you have empathy for
everyone but yourself.

too many times,

you've drowned yourself for people who can't swim in your love language. burned yourself for people who can't put out their own flames. abandoned yourself for people who pick and choose when to open their doors to you. too many times, you've put yourself last.

you deserve days and nights that don't involve
you being at war with your mirror.

you deserve days and nights that don't involve your
self-esteem holding your energy hostage.

you deserve days and nights that don't involve
your parents' trauma taking center stage.

you deserve love.

(different stages of your life will come with different familiarity and different understanding, but your growth doesn't owe anyone an explanation or an apology)

people will stop understanding you at certain phases of your life. growth comes in different forms so sometimes it's harder to recognize. but you can never take it personally if you've outgrown their comfort level of you. you are a version of themselves they are yet to meet.

koigu.

oxymoron.

silence can be both
healing and toxic,
but never at the same time.

(it's not about what you can do for me when we're together, it's about what you can do for yourself)

i don't need you to love my flaws,
i do that for myself already.
all i require is that you **love your own.**

koigu.

sometimes,

we think it's the connection ending that hurts, when in truth, it's the thought of the time you spent with them that hurts. it's the thought of the energy you spent on them that hurts. the intimacy, the memories, the nostalgia. if it was real, the love will always remain.

faux angels.

be wary of those who only encourage you to chase your dreams when it's convenient for them. the ones who want you to chase your dreams until it threatens their ego. the ones who encourage you to chase your dreams as long as it doesn't displace them from your priorities. **be wary**.

<u>*shallow realizations.*</u>

don't spend too long swimming in the idea
that it'll never go back to the way it was
when it's time to accept that this is the
way that it's meant to be.
people grow closer and apart,
situations change and unfold,
love evolves and connection changes,
but regret is easy to drown in.

(to whomever finds this)

there's nothing wrong with having expectations, and when someone doesn't live up to what they said they would do, there is nothing wrong with holding them accountable. love doesn't excuse broken promises and erase pain—**you deserve connections that admit when they've fallen short.**

*(never let loyalty force you into obligation. never let loyalty make you
forget where home is)*

are you loyal to you as much as you are loyal to other people?
or does your loyalty not understand what reciprocation is yet?

brittle.

connections born out of convenience have no backbone. they
are fragile, break easily, and don't offer support when you
truly need it. don't block the path for fulfilling energy to reach
you by continuously entertaining hollow connections.

koigu.

*(give me the chance to figure things out on my own before stepping
in and trying to save the day. give me the freedom to make my own
mistakes before trying to figure out a solution for my plight. give me the
space to navigate through obstacles without trying to give me direction)*

be there for me,
but give me the freedom to be there for myself.

listen

to your sadness. pay attention to what it's trying to say instead of blocking its voice or ignoring its advances. you don't have to give it permanence, only time, patience, and ears. once it's told you what it has to say, escort it out gently to make room for happiness.

koigu.

(how you see yourself is more important than how anyone else sees you)

i used to choose to see myself through the eyes of lovers who viewed me as unlovable. lovers who asked me to tuck my flaws away as if they made me look sloppy and undesirable. now, the only eyes that i choose to see myself through are my own.

(it's simple)

some lovers hear,
better lovers **listen**.

koigu.

sometimes,

it's not that you lost something because you learned a lesson too late;
sometimes you just outgrow what you thought was once meant for
you and that lesson no longer becomes applicable.

funny truths.

i feel bad for the ones who thought they
knew me better than i know myself.
truth is, i haven't even bloomed into my full form yet,
so i guess the joke is on you.

**oversell.**

stop using time as a measuring tool for
where you should be in your life.

stop using time as a measuring tool for what should stay in your life.

stop using time as a measuring tool for
what shouldn't stay in your life.

stop using time as a measuring tool.

(try not to torture yourself so frequently)

you take a gulp of poison every time you swallow your pride for someone who consistently can't do the same for you.

koigu.

feather weight.

appreciate the ones who carry your concerns
when your soul feels heavy.
the ones who put their load down for a brief moment
to check in on you and make you feel lighter. the ones
who resist from weighing you down with their opinion
but instead offer you a space free of judgment.

unfinished.

there is more to your story.
you may have put the book down for a brief moment,
or you may be stuck on a chapter that is hard to digest,
you may have paper cuts from flipping past pages too fast,
or you may not even know how to begin,
but there is still much more to your story.

koigu.

*(love and location have nothing to do with each other. i can have love
for you and still keep you at bay)*

i still love you quietly.
not as loudly as you may like,
but i still love you.

darling,

i hope you look back at all of your mistakes with love. regret has a funny way of transforming itself into resentment if you're not careful.

(i hope you realize that you are deserving of the same space that you afford them)

you take on so much.
more than you can handle,
more than they know you can handle,
and then you wonder why
you never have any room left for yourself.

gentle reminder:

it does get better. sometimes just not in the way you expect or in the way you think you deserve, but it does get better. sometimes you have to feel a little trapped until you feel free, a little lost until you find your way, a little helpless until the waves settle.

unconquerable.

there is no connection more powerful than two people
bringing their individualities to the table
with no intention of diluting each other's essence, but instead,
celebrating what makes each other unique.

delayed understandings.

when you've forgotten how many chances you've given them, sometimes it's a mark of how forgiving and full of love you are, but other times, it's a gentle reminder telling you that you probably should've left a long time ago.

koigu.

(it all starts with you)

connections flow more when you stop looking
at people as a source of happiness.

when you stop attaching expectations to anyone's
capability or inability to love you.

when you stop dipping your toes in water that feels cold
and become the source you've always needed.

a love that holds your hand on your bad days and
weak moments and tells you that it knows you deeper
than you're feeling about yourself right now.

a love that reassures you that even though you may
be in a place of darkness, you are still seen.

a judgment-free kind of love.

broken obligations.

you don't have to reserve a space of love for people who
think they are entitled to your energy by association.

you don't have to commit to a consistent act of patience
with those who use your energy like playdough.

you don't have to familiarize yourself with silence
to give someone else's truth a voice.

(take whatever necessary measures you need to reclaim yourself)

healthy hiatuses.
healthy breaks.
healthy boundaries.
healthy connections.
healthy love.

koigu.

it's okay,

it wasn't for you. now watch as that vacant space gets filled by what you actually deserve.

stumbling steps.

i want to practice your love language like a
dancer practices their pirouettes;
i hope i never fall, but if i ever do,
i hope you hold a cup of patience for me
as i practice until i get it right.

koigu.

(poison comes in the form of denial. at times, accepting things for what they are will give you the freedom and peace that you never thought existed)

you hold on to connections that you feel disconnected from,
and then you wonder why you feel so disconnected from yourself.
sometimes self-love comes in the form of admittance—
admittance that no matter how long or strongly you hold on,
you can never force growth in a connection.

(changing yourself to suit me doesn't suit me)

if you ever have the temptation to change yourself just for me,
just know that i was never for you to begin with.

if anything,
my presence should encourage you to show up as your full self,
not who you think i desire for you to be.

koigu.

smoother surroundings.

putting resistance toward anything outgrowing you
only adds friction to your own growth.
let it outgrow you,
don't prolong its inevitable departure,
something better will find you.

(it is never your responsibility to convince someone of their worth.
it is never your responsibility to convince someone of the beauty they
possess. it is never your responsibility to place cushions down for their
self-esteem)

self-esteem is a heavy thing to carry. it's an even heavier thing to carry
when you're carrying it around for a lover who doesn't see the beauty
and magic that you see in them.

koigu.

intrinsic perceptions.

be appreciated beyond your vessel.

in ways that go deeper than the wars you carry on your skin.

beyond the superficial reminders the mirror
gives you not to accept yourself.

away from mouths that have made your name a home
because they aren't brave enough to sing their own.

(be more gentle with yourself)

flowers will grow from your mistakes.

koigu.

notes on healing:

healing is a sloppy and reckless affair.
you will fall back into several habits unintentionally,
break things that you believed you were in the process of fixing,
play games of hide-and-seek with self-love and your ego,
but this process is so necessary.

(practice honesty, constantly. practice honesty with yourself, consistently)

honesty is like cardio for the soul.

koigu.

(consistency as a love language)

some people

we must simply stop giving the power to hurt us by choosing not to
allow their consistently inconsistent actions.

awareness shift.

people who don't know what they want usually
hurt people who know what they want.
so if you ever find yourself holding on to someone that is unsure
of your energy and what you have to offer, release yourself
from them so you can make room for what is ready for you.

koigu.

(i see more than i say)

do not mistake my gentleness for passiveness.
the lack of words is not a lack of awareness.

darling,

your pockets are full of keys that belong to homes in other people,
but why do you consistently lose the one that belongs to your own?

koigu.

<u>*road signs.*</u>

you can take many routes to get to my heart,
but by far the quickest way there is through my mind.

never ending destinations.

inner peace doesn't have a finish line. the journey to attain it never ends, but that's the beauty in it. you learn from the moments of chaos and confusion so you can truly appreciate the waves of calm and happiness.

but you see,

it could never work if your ego was louder than the love you have for me.

bitter days.

on some days,
you will feel more fragile than you do on others.
allow yourself to break.
allow yourself to sink.
allow yourself to retreat.
you are allowed days like these;
days to feel,
days to recluse,
days to process.
tomorrow will taste much **sweeter**.

koigu.

(arrivals and departures)

sometimes people stay,
physically but not emotionally.
and sometimes people leave,
emotionally but not physically.

damask.

you see,

self-love is a long dance
that you will
routinely fall out of rhythm with,
forget the steps to,
and struggle to master,
but no one said practicing
this dance would be easy.

damask.

to whomever finds this;

lowering your frequency by matching their energy will only leave you at risk of doing things that you don't recognize and attracting things that don't belong to you. not every situation requires for you to be a mirror so that you can be understood.

divine communication.

conversations that feel like a cleanse,
conversations that give you oxygen,
conversations that feel like water,
conversations that give you life,
intentional conversations,
you are worthy of that.

damask.

(if you nurture the connection i have with myself, you can stay as long as you like)

i don't measure the strength of my connections
off of what people can do for me,
i measure them off which connections allow me
to stay most connected to my(self).

your ripening will take time. the sweetness from your growth will require patience to taste. you are no ordinary thing—**don't expect your bloom to be similar to theirs.**

damask.

(give it as much time as it needs to find you)

not everyone you're ready for will be ready for you.
the energy you possess, the passion you possess,
the love you possess.
not everyone will be ready for the light
that beams and magic that spills from your chest.
do not let impatience or loneliness lower your standards.

permanent winds.

i have the energy for a lot of things,
but when i stop having the energy for you,
it's hard to get that energy back.

damask.

darling,

asking for a lover who understands you, when you haven't spent the
time trying to understand yourself, only puts people in your path who
mirror the energy that you're giving off. become that lover first and
attract the energy that you reflect.

i'm more concerned with whether you enjoy being around yourself, rather than whether you enjoy being around me.

—a connection free from attachment

damask.

(don't show resistance when the universe is asking you to let go)

you will stop being for certain people in particular phases of their life. accept their transition, applaud their growth, and allow separation to happen naturally no matter how painful it may be. **you have a journey of your own to focus on.**

unattached.

teach me about myself.
not just about the light,
but about the dark.
but realize that it is not your duty
to be the balance between the two for me.
understand that your only duty is to love yourself deeply,
and maybe on my low days,
that can inspire me to do the same.

damask.

expired.

the version of who you were before doesn't interest me as much as the version of yourself that you are currently and the version of yourself that you are trying to become. having a heavy past doesn't mean that you are not worth acceptance or forgiveness.

sometimes,

your true power lies in your ability to surrender to what you can't control.

damask.

overflow.

when you see happiness dripping from their pores,
remember that holding a cup out to try and gather
what you see will never make that happiness your own.

happiness will find you,
but drop the idea that it can only be through other people.

(acceptance can be beautiful and freeing)

if you keep reminiscing on what was good,
will you ever leave what is bad?
it's okay to see things for what they are now
instead of romanticizing old experiences
and using memories to justify not leaving.

exhaustion.

even the most patient people get tired of understanding
when you push them to their limit.

even the most patient people get tired of listening
when you push them to their limit.

even the most patient people get tired.

(your layers make you limitless)

how beautiful it is to know yourself,
but know that there are still many parts to
you that you are yet to discover.

damask.

true love knows when to let go,
but true love also knows when to adapt.
to situations,
to change,
to shifts in energy and languages,
to mistakes,
to growth.
true love knows when to adapt,
but only you have the power to decide
who and what is worth changing your fabric for.

(sometimes, it's a shift in perspective that changes the way the music around you sounds)

there are keys to life's melodies that i am still not familiar with. keys that i may have heard before, or keys that i am only being introduced to now, but one thing i am certain of is that i am the musician behind the keys, and i determine how the music in my life sounds.

damask.

(going forward)

keep watering yourself until you feel like you again.

reminder:

some doors come disguised as opportunities because
they don't seem to have a lock attached to them,
but just because a door is easy to open doesn't
mean that it's meant for you.

damask.

<u>signs of struggle.</u>

i have survived many internal wars
that no one knew i was fighting,
survived many battles that threatened
to bring me out of my element,
so if you ever see a smile on my face
or hear laughter coming from my direction,
understand that these are **reminders** of my victories

(take your dear sweet time)

this masterpiece that you are becoming,
don't let anyone rush you into becoming it.

damask.

(you matter too. your energy, your concerns, your thoughts. you
don't have to sit your emotions in the backseat because no one else is
accommodating them)

you sympathize with everyone so much
and empathize with yourself so little,
and with time,
i hope you learn to stop running away from yourself
when the thing you need the most is **you.**

doses of honey.

be nice to your wounds. some are still waiting to be heard out,
some are still waiting for ears that listen.
some always find themselves on the cusp of closing,
and others are a little more stubborn and need to reopen to be seen.
be nice to your wounds—some are still healing.

damask.

dense expectations.

i'm learning to disassociate myself from who
and what people expect me to be.

it's too wearing.

it's too heavy.

don't add weight to my bag because i am not who you want me to be.

that is not my responsibility.

(it's going to take time. it's going to take a really long time)

you will run out of patience with yourself several times in your healing. you will tire of how you break and mend repeatedly, how you soften and harden religiously, how you shift between self-acceptance and self-resentment, but you deserve nothing but love throughout.

damask.

(it might've been for you at some point and now it isn't, but that's okay)

there's humility in accepting the things that are not for you anymore. it takes a real quieting of the ego for you to hear the universe telling you that you are deserving of better energy.

mantra;

where you are planted
is not where you
have to remain rooted.

damask.

(you need yourself sometimes too)

do not blame your body for not having the energy to fight other people's battles anymore; welcome your body back to the realization that you deserve to fight your own battles too.

to whom this may concern: you don't have to continuously be harsh on yourself, pouring salt on wounds that aren't open to healing yet. you're doing the best that you can. let no one's happiness or contentment discourage you because you haven't found your own. it will find you.

to whom this may concern: second chances are a choice and a privilege. you choose what you allow and what you don't, but never let anyone dictate whether or not you should keep their energy around when it affects your well-being. no one owns your peace but you.

to whom this may concern: sometimes, searching for old feelings in old places won't make you feel like your old self again. sometimes, accepting that you've shed old skin and that you're deserving of a better version than your older self is what will make you feel like you again.

damask.

<u>lost maps.</u>

if someone is lost,
the best place you can ever lead them
is back to themselves.

understand;

announcing all of your moves doesn't make them more impactful.
sometimes the real magic happens in silence.

damask.

(discern the difference)

are you not explaining it well,
or do they just not hear you
the way you want to be heard?

lately,

you've been swimming in sadness, not because you want to, but because sadness is all you've known. i know the shore might feel too far from your comfort zone right now, but you should know that even the water you're most familiar with can eventually drown you too.

damask.

(not everyone who waters you is good for you)

you flow differently when the right people are watering you.

the greatest lesson you ever taught me is never to oversell my worth.

i guess love has a way of making you feel a lot of things. sometimes, love has a way of making you feel many things all at once. other times, love has a humbling way of making you feel absolutely nothing because you've felt too much for too long, and you're tired of feeling. but by far one of the strangest things love does is inject you with this undeniably vast ocean filled with benefit of the doubt. benefit of the doubt that can turn into resentment if love isn't watered the way it's supposed to be—in your love language. reciprocation can take many forms, but if it happens in a way that you can't understand, then it becomes an uphill battle. i lost my legs running it. in a battle not to lose my mind as well, i'm slowly learning that the ones who truly see you won't need a light beam, a candle, moonlight, or an excuse—they will just see you, and see you for you, and you will never have any reason to doubt it.

damask.

sometimes,

it's not a question of "why won't they change?" instead, it's a question of "why am i trying to change them?" stop trying to mold people into versions of themselves that are close to a level of growth and healing you yourself have reached—give their bloom time.

(what a selfish thing it is, not to be honest with yourself)

is your happiness really yours, or does it belong to everyone who thinks you're happy when you're truly not? facades are easy to pull, but you can never trick your soul.

you don't have to overstay your welcome if their home is full of pain and consistent triggering of your trauma. just because they welcomed you in with open arms initially doesn't mean the space that you occupy is still welcoming—to your growth, to your ideas, to your identity, to your love, to you. connections change, energy changes, some people grow, and some people don't, but you don't owe anyone a prolonged period of your presence just because they were once there for you. accept what has turned toxic without trying to sweeten what doesn't sit well with your soul anymore. the keys to your happiness belong in your pockets and nobody else's. **there's no late fees worse than the ones that tax your soul.**

reminder:

be careful how you place deadlines and timelines on your dreams.
does it come from a place of wanting to challenge
and push yourself to reach your goal?
or does it come from a place of fear and impatience?
what's for you will never escape you, and
what escapes you isn't for you.

damask.

(there are reasons why you are in their life too)

we spend countless time wondering why we attract certain people in
our lives
but never really ask ourselves why certain people attract us.

a lover who helps you unlock beautiful new layers to yourself.

one who doesn't try to erase parts of your
essence so they can color in their own.

one who doesn't take away from who you are but supports
your metamorphosis through all of your phases.

you deserve that.

damask.

__evolutions.__

you are a beautiful living thing.

let the love you have for yourself evolve as well.

how you watered yourself yesterday may not necessarily
be the way you need to water yourself tomorrow.

let the love you have for yourself be flexible
enough to outstand any unexpected winds.

(know what you deserve)

never confuse contentment with happiness.
just because you have the capacity to accept it
doesn't mean that it is what you deserve.

damask.

darling,

please remember that it is not your duty to heal me. you can love me through my healing if you want, but remember that your first duty always remains with you.

(to whom this may concern)

it's all love,
even if you outgrow me.

one day,

you will grow tired of over-explaining yourself to the people committed to misunderstanding you. one day, you will say nothing, and you will let your growth speak for itself.

lessons learned:

if i'm not for you,
i will not spend time and energy trying to be.
my truth is worth too much for me just to betray in favor of your ego.

damask.

(never become a prisoner to an apology)

never let an apology erode away the accountability that should be attached to someone's actions. an apology is easy to make; actions are harder to rectify.

perfect footing.

what i left behind is not better than what is in front of me.
what is in front of me is not more important than what i have already.
my placement in this very moment is not by coincidence;
where i am currently is exactly where i need to be.

damask.

to whomever finds this:

don't fumble your blessings chasing what isn't meant for you.

(open your heart)

it's never too late to listen to the parts of you that you ignored when you weren't seeing yourself in true light or loving yourself in the way you deserve to be loved. give those parts the chance to speak, the chance to be heard, the chance to be felt, without interruption.

damask.

(you will keep repeating the same cycles over and over until you really deal with whatever it is that you need to deal with)

you can never fake your growth;
your triggers will always expose you.

but you see,

home is not a place, it's a feeling. so if you ever feel lost, retreat back to you and spend more time with yourself. there are answers that exist within you that you may have ignored for too long.

damask.

the goal;

is not to try to resonate with every single thing and every single person. the goal is to find things and experiences that help you resonate more with your(self).

low phases.

understand that whatever you're going through currently is temporary.

understand that whatever you're scared to face has no power over you, but only the power you give it.

understand that whatever you're scared to lose shouldn't scare you as much as the idea of losing yourself.

damask.

(you are deserving too)

you owe yourself the same time and patience
that you give so freely to the ones who consistently let you down.

(love isn't a game, neither is it a competition)

a true lover is not looking to compete with you. a true lover wants to see you elevate yourself through the things that ignite you and make you happy, without attaching their personal growth to everything happening with yours. they'll never look to dim your light so they can shine theirs.

damask.

<u>reversal.</u>

give yourself time to unlearn the habits you
don't resonate with anymore.
the ones you picked up when you dropped the
cup of love you have for yourself.
the ones you adopted out of sympathy for everyone
else and lack of empathy for yourself.
give yourself time to unlearn.

your healing will involve a lot of forgiving,

forgiving of yourself.

damask.

(never betray yourself by consistently explaining yourself to people who have ears that are permanently on mute)

some people make their minds up about what you have to say before you have spoken a word, and i hope you learn to discern between those who challenge your thoughts because they want to understand better and the ones who only listen with the intent of disagreeing with you.

they don't make lovers like you anymore;

a lover who can pour into your cup but make sure their own isn't empty, a lover who sees freedom as a requirement and not as a threat, a lover who is forgiving but still knows their worth. never settle for less than you deserve.

damask.

**broken mirrors.**

you won't be recognizable to
many people through your healing.
equally through your healing,
a lot of people won't be recognizable to you.

priorities.

tend to your garden first before you tend to mine;
i promise you i won't take it personally.
flowers will still bloom on my side even when you're focusing on you.

damask.

understand this:

growth looks different on everyone;
you can never dress it up for me.

(give yourself the kickstart you deserve)

your healing doesn't need to begin once you get that apology.

your healing doesn't need to begin once you get that closure.

your healing doesn't need to begin once you get that explanation.

your healing can begin where you are, right now,
without anyone's approval or authority.

i hope

you never feel guilt for exercising your boundaries even if they don't understand why. even if your answers or actions don't appease their ego. even if they view it as malicious without having a scope into your inner world. you have a responsibility to honor yourself.

changes.

you're a multidimensional being.
you could never be loved in just one way.
you're constantly evolving,
so the love for yourself will evolve too.
there is no wrong in wanting to be loved
in a language that is fluent to your soul.

damask.

listen:

never try to force me into your vibration
if we're not on the same wave.
every ocean is different,
and you're not obliged to swim in one
that feels uncomfortable for you,
and neither am i.

to whom this may concern: running away and distancing yourself from everything might camouflage your pain for a brief period of time, but you can only hide yourself from the truth for so long before it turns its lights on and makes itself seen.

to whom this may concern: your value runs much deeper than the shallow oceans people have placed around you—you don't have to swim in them. you can stop living in line with people's expectations of you and drop all the weight they attached to you without your permission.

to whom this may concern: people will only meet you at a level they are familiar with. people will only meet you at a level they are comfortable with. you can never move or push anyone to reach a level that you understand, no matter how much you want them to. accept or release.

to whom this may concern: embrace the shifts and shake hands with what needs to change. embrace the energy you can't control and find acceptance for feelings that don't want to stay. don't allow holding on to become second nature because you're not used to anything good staying.

to whom this may concern: some people show you what they want to show you, and other people show you what they might not want to but what you need to see. intention means nothing if there is truth lacking behind it.

to whom this may concern: not knowing where to turn isn't the end. not knowing where to navigate doesn't mean that you're lost. not knowing how to look forward doesn't mean that you're taking steps back. not knowing how to ask for help doesn't mean that you're not worthy of it.

damask.

(some of your hardest days will be the ones you have to go through alone)

self-love will feel lonely at times,
but sometimes holding your own hand
will feel a lot warmer than having it held by someone else.

slow down,

sometimes we become so desperate for change that we start to sabotage all the work that we've put into ourselves already. this new version of you will require time, it will require softness, it will require patience—stop rushing its arrival.

damask.

(how it goes)

you stop searching for it,
and then, suddenly, it finds you.

(the most beautiful gift you could ever give yourself is one of self-love)

i carry the same joy a child finds in a new toy
when i find new ways to love myself.

charmeuse.

balance.

do not waste chapters in your life trying to get even.

do not waste ink trying to rewrite someone's narrative of you.

do not continuously give energy to what depletes you.

do not say much on it if nothing's to be said.

just let the universe do its thing.

<u>*sufficient.*</u>

a life constantly lived trying to be enough for other people
is exhausting. eventually i hope you learn to breathe,
choose yourself, and realize that as long as you're enough
for yourself, you'll never need to overpour in someone
else's cup to keep them around or keep them happy.

gentle reminder:

small steps are still steps.
never undermine the progress you've made because
the footprints you see are not big enough to make
an impression on where you want to be.

**rinse & repeat.**

one of the most harmful things you can ever do is constantly and consistently run back into cycles that you have already identified. sometimes what's comfortable may feel the easiest, but what's easiest isn't always what's best for you. shift yourself from what keeps you stuck.

the more you fall in love with yourself, the more i fall in love with you.

—*a love free from attachment*

charmeuse.

understand this:

you will never complete anyone by dismantling yourself just to fit the version of you that they desire. real love has no desire to change you, but simply to watch, admire, encourage, and hold your hand as you grow through the changes that you, yourself, wish to facilitate.

the most difficult conversations that you will ever have will be with yourself.

the most difficult choices you make will sometimes be internally by yourself.

the hardest person you're ever going to have to be honest with is yourself: **flowers bloom from honesty you water yourself with.**

charmeuse.

**monotony.**

you will have many quiet revolutions.

muted applause in the shadows.

silent transitions with beautiful outcomes.

it will look uneventful at times,
it will feel pointless in moments,
but this is healing,
this is growth.

fresh surroundings.

you were not meant to be stuck in the healing phase. don't let the familiarity of the process fool you into thinking that there is always going to be gold where you've cultivated safety before. **heal, learn,** and **shift** into spaces that encourage healthy growth.

charmeuse.

(effective communication peels layers open sharper than any knife could)

discuss love languages early in a connection.
lay foundation down for how you wish to be loved,
but also set the energy for what you won't allow.
sometimes the sparks we set
turn into wildfires because we refused to pour water
on what we knew wasn't for us to begin with.

where your brain is at is more important to me than where your hands are at.

—*intimacy*

old clothing.

some connections will start to feel like an
undersized shirt as you grow,
but feel no guilt for choosing not to wear
what doesn't fit your soul anymore.
expiration dates are common in connections,
but the connection you have with yourself should never expire.

indifferent bonds.

i've never really believed that similarities are
what make people soul mates.
sometimes it's the differences,
and the ability to make flowers bloom in spite of them,
that truly make two people connected.
sometimes it's deeper than how you resonate,
and all about what you learn.

charmeuse.

(pointing fingers is easy, looking within can be the harder route, but it's only when you start taking accountability for your actions that you truly begin to emancipate yourself. it's only when you start to take responsibility for your actions that you truly begin to see yourself. it's only when you stop hiding from the truth that the answers you've been looking for start to find you)

the shoe fits differently when you start holding yourself accountable.

(we all have our own journeys; let them map out the way they should)

let people learn their lesson the way they're
supposed to learn their lesson
without you trying to impose a lesson that you learned on them.

understand:

i could never be the space that heals you,
that responsibility does not belong to me.
all i want is to be the space that encourages
you to find healing for yourself.

(there's magic in your bones, believe it)

things become easier when you drown away the idea of perfection.

when you slowly wash away the idea that there is a certain
standard that you have to exhibit to be enough.

things become easier when you accept your own magic
and resist from comparing it to anyone else's.

charmeuse.

__return to sender.__

you've remained soft when you've been given every reason not to.

exercised patience when you've had the right to demand more.

loved when the ones you loved weren't deserving of your warmth.

you've forgotten about you too often and maybe
it's time to channel that energy back home.

(regardless of how different our journeys may be, my intentions were always pure)

my love doesn't go anywhere,
my energy just changes direction.

charmeuse.

sometimes,

soul mates are revealed when you stop viewing them romantically.
when your lens is not tinted by courtship
but cleared by true friendship.

timely.

nothing forced into existence ever lasts.

all the glue and temporary effort put into making
it stick will always peel off eventually.

allow the things meant for you to come freely to you.

with no friction or opposition, with no rush
or restlessness, with just **patience**.

charmeuse.

mantra;

i will find what i need
when i need it the most.

(energy you deserve)

tell me your triggers
so i can navigate carefully through the trauma
and hold your hand while you find a place of healing,
kind of love.

charmeuse.

(this journey will have many highs and lows, many dips and turns, but this is how it will have to be as you find your way back to yourself)

reclaiming yourself will take time.
stepping back into your power will take time.
unlearning what you thought was true and
relearning to be gentle with the opinion you
have of yourself will take time.
unearth yourself slowly; you deserve patience and all of that time.

darling,

this happiness was meant to find you. don't resist the waves.

charmeuse.

(practice this over and over until what you can control is back in your grasp again)

make a habit of surrendering and letting go of what you can't control.

projections are louder than bombs.

for too long you misinterpreted my energy, but i promise you, it was not because of any fault of your own. i guess inconsistency has a way of breeding a consistency of confusion, and that was the theme park i unknowingly built around your emotions. for too long, you felt out of sync with my energy because i brought habits from my past into our connection, and maybe all our connection ever needed was openness so you could see that my bad habits had nothing to do with you. vulnerability was the hardest wall i ever had to break down and seeing the traces of debris on the ground always scared me. i guess the scariest thing about it all was that it served as a reminder that even through my resiliency i can still be fragile, i can still need a helping hand, i can still be vulnerable. and maybe that's exactly what was missing from our connection—vulnerability. maybe it wasn't that i found you at a time when you had more love for me; maybe it was that i found you at a time when my ego was louder than any kind of love i had for you, and i never gave you the chance to hear it.

connections that don't ask you to bite your tongue.

connections that don't require you to hide to be seen.

connections that don't fear your opinion.

connections that never look at disagreement
or indifference as a threat.

connections like this.

(i hope you realize that the lack of footsteps is not a lack of progression. growth isn't always tangible, it isn't always something that is apparent or visible, but just because you don't see where you're going or know how you're going to get there, it doesn't mean that you eventually won't. magic is always happening behind the scenes and your angels are always working in your favor. return the favor by offering your patience. all the goodness you've been waiting for will soon be in your reach)

maybe **you're not stuck**. maybe you're meant to be rooted where you are for the time being. maybe there is still much to be learned in this current phase that you are anchored in. maybe where you are currently is exactly where you need to be so you can get to where you want to be.

charmeuse.

gentle reminder:

the universe reacts to your intentions, not the opinions others have of you; **remember that.**

safe keeping.

the thing about being too passive, too consistently, is that
you form an unhealthy habit of brushing off accountability.
you find yourself with unresolved pain that has piled up
somewhere in you because you've sacrificed your truth
once too many times. **your truth deserves protection**.

charmeuse.

acclamation.

never let lack of applause fool you into thinking
that what you're doing isn't important.
never let absence of celebration fool you into thinking
that you're not worthy of occupying spaces with love.
external validation is easy to get;
learn to **honor you and your flowers first**.

but you see,

you could never replicate the aura of a
woman who knows her purpose.
it runs deeper than what you see. she's done
soul work; you can never imitate that.

charmeuse.

(listening, but really listening. with intention, with openness, no distractions, just love)

active listening as a love language.

contrasts.

that thing that makes you unique,
don't dilute it for anyone who doesn't
like how sweet it tastes.
don't drown it for anyone who doesn't
know how to swim in its depths.
don't throw it away for anyone who doesn't
know what gold looks like.
your difference deserves celebration.

wholeness.

there is nothing fulfilling about being appreciated or valued
in pockets. eventually you learn the difference between
the people that don't have time and the ones that don't
want to make time. the lines may be thin, but you don't
have to exist where intentions are gray or blurry.

but,

is it really love if it fears your freedom?
if the thought of space causes concern?
if the idea of you growing wings is greeted with a pair of scissors?
if your existence is the glue that holds their identity together?
is it really, love?

charmeuse.

(quite simple)

if my growth intimidates you,
then you are not focused on
your own journey enough.

reminder:

you will always know how healthy a connection
is for you by how you feel after interactions.
not just in the sweet moments, but in the rough too.
energy lingers, but it also never lies.

charmeuse.

(soul exchange)

hold me accountable so i know it's real.
hold yourself accountable so i know you're real.

secrets about me:

if it's not feeding my happiness or my growth,
then i'd rather not sit at its table for too long.

charmeuse.

don't take it personally,

when i say that you could never attract a love like mine until you love yourself,
because you can never attract what you're not ready for.

(it doesn't lose its sacredness just because you are keeping it to yourself for now)

it is not malicious to keep good news to yourself. sometimes, protecting your energy involves holding on to things that are important to you because not everyone has the same intentions you have with your blessings. **envy comes in many disguises**.

healing involves taking responsibility for ways in which you've let yourself down as well.

not in a way of guilting yourself for the times you didn't love yourself the way you needed to, but in a way of acknowledging any parts of you that may still feel heavy.

forgive yourself.

*(do not hold yourself prisoner to the mistakes you made in the past. you
still deserve love, even in your lowest moments)*

give yourself permission to make mistakes,
but don't give your mistakes permission to turn into resentment.
you deserve to learn from everything you've encountered
without attaching more heaviness to your bag.

charmeuse.

lessons learned:

communication and consistency are like
food and water in a connection.

(choose wisely)

every time you choose love, you win.

every time you choose peace, you win.

every time you choose yourself, you win.

charmeuse.

(everyone deserves peace, and you are no different)

heal the parts of you that hold resentment for
being forced to grow up too fast,
for having to pick up responsibility where others should have,
for shrinking yourself and packaging your
self-esteem so others may rise.
your inner child deserves peace.

**selflessness.**

love has no bounds when the self-love is genuine on both ends.
you pour into you, i pour into me,
and through that we find ways to pour back into each other.
how could we ever lose?

charmeuse.

rebirth.

there are certain parts of me that are slowly dying,
but there is nothing sad about it,
because there are even more beautiful parts
of me that are being birthed.

(much different)

some connections feel like work,
other connections feel like the water you
drink after you've put in some work.

charmeuse.

(flowers will grow from this)

whatever you are currently unlearning does not define you.

how long it is taking for you to reach a place of internal comfort does not define you either.

you will take many routes in your healing,
but with love and patience,
all of them will eventually **lead you back to yourself.**

(the energy will always tell you what isn't for you anymore)

the energy will always be different when you
revisit a place you've outgrown,
the energy will always be different if you
reexplore a person you've outgrown,
the energy will always be different when you take steps back
to reach someone at a level you don't resonate with anymore.

charmeuse.

healthy friendship.

true friendship never looks at your progress as competition.

true friendship doesn't look at your endeavors with envy.

true friendship celebrates your steps no matter
how big or small they may be
and finds inspiration where they may feel they are lacking.

(hidden talents)

being misunderstood and knowing that it has
nothing to do with you is a **superpower.**

(you deserve goodness too)

you poison yourself slowly when you consistently hold space for those who aren't holding the same space for you. there is nothing fulfilling about unrequited energy. reciprocation isn't everything, but you deserve to feel the waves you give off come back to you from time to time.

hard pills and soft pillows.

you can be upset about the timing,
or you can be thankful for the lessons
that you will learn while you wait for it to manifest.
one choice feels softer than the other.

charmeuse.

if you outgrow me, i'm genuinely happy for you because that means that we've learned everything that we need to learn from our connection.

—*healthy endings/beginnings*

(start today)

choosing yourself can be a struggle, especially if you've been conditioned to choose others from the time you were younger, but it's never too late to start now. it's never too late to prioritize yourself, even if tending to you seems unfamiliar and foreign at first.

charmeuse.

(never send your intuition to voicemail)

there is no betrayal worse than ignoring your own intuition.

(you are not an apology letter; don't treat yourself like one)

apologizing for how you expressed yourself in moments that you recognize you were operating at a low vibration, is awareness.

apologizing for how you expressed yourself in moments where you had the right to feel the way you feel in fear of a negative reaction, is a trauma response.

charmeuse.

(your concerns are not made less valid by their inability to fully comprehend how you feel)

their reaction to you
holding them accountable
is not your burden to carry.

good omens:

identifying cycles before they begin again
is a sign that you are stepping back into your power.

charmeuse.

beautiful ignorance.

if you were competing with me in any capacity,
i wouldn't have a clue because i am too busy
watering the flowers in my own garden to even notice.

growth:

it's nice when people can see how much you've grown,
but what's even more beautiful is when you realize
how much you've grown without their words or validation.

eventually,

you will grow tired of continuing to celebrate those who have never listened or danced to any beats your heart gives off. resentment builds in funny ways and sometimes a lack of reciprocation is the seed that starts it all. plant your feet in healthier spaces.

(creating distance as a form of self-care)

not everything is a trauma response.
sometimes your intuition and discernment
are at work,
and what you're doing is actually
what is best for you,
your mental health,
and your peace of mind.

charmeuse.

for too long,

you've clapped for people who have kept their hands in their pockets when good things happen to you, and i hope you find the awareness to move to where you feel synergy in how you're appreciated.

(true connection goes far beyond)

the highest form of connection goes beyond how romantic or platonic it is.

when they can see your worth without letting your flaws change their perspective, **that's love**.

when they encourage you to show up fully for yourself despite other people's perspectives, **that's love**.

sabbatical.

absence may make the heart grow fonder, but sometimes what absence does is reveal the true nature of your relationship with certain people. some people will hold resentment or envy from afar, but show love and share smiles up close. time always unmasks who isn't healthy for you.

(you are worthy just the way you are)

convincing people of your worthiness is exhausting.
your spirit will eventually get tired of running the distance
for people who aren't even waiting for you at the finish line.

charmeuse.

every road you take that leads you back to yourself is worth the mileage.

—*healing*

necessary revelations.

don't be upset that they showed you who they truly are,
be grateful that you now have the awareness
to move forward with no illusions.

charmeuse.

(show yourself kindness by planting yourself where love exists)

kindness is still poison to a toxic person.
never overextend yourself in spaces where
people are committed to misunderstanding your intent.

mantra;

who i used to be
isn't more important
than who i am currently
and who i am shaping up to be.

charmeuse.

(happiness exists in this space)

lower the volume on needing to be understood,
and increase the intention to understand yourself better.

sweet seclusion.

there will be days when disappearing feels lighter than showing up,
days when silence shifts you more than words,
days when solitude fills your cup more than anyone else's presence.
there will be days when you need you more than anything else,
and there is nothing wrong in that.

charmeuse.

(nothing feels better than finally giving yourself what you should've been giving yourself all along)

being loved feels warm.
loving yourself feels like
the entire sun inside of you.

tears,

sometimes they flow because the hurt knows no other way to express itself. sometimes they flow so you can finally let go and release. other times they flow because they are meant to water beautiful new beginnings.

charmeuse.

(you can never lose whenever you're being completely honest with yourself)

you can dress your wounds in whatever clothing you desire,
but one day you will run out of things to put on and be left
naked with nothing but truth to confront.

**final installments.**

forgiveness may look like moving on to the next chapter
and anticipating what the other pages have to offer,
but sometimes forgiveness means closing that book
and deciding never to read it again.

charmeuse.

(keep that fire burning)

being you
will be too bright for some people;
it will be too blinding,
it will be too hard to contain.
they would rather you were a small lightbulb
when you are meant to be an entire flame.

(be unstoppable)

you are truly unstoppable when you know yourself beyond
their projections, their opinions, and their indifferences.
you add an extra layer of protection when you choose to
love yourself through their misunderstandings of you.

charmeuse.

reminder:

every time you choose yourself, you apply a
thick layer of balm to your spirit.

(softness looks good on you)

the best revenge is
choosing to remain soft
even when you have every
reason not to

landing.

landing.

life has no particular order. it has no correct sequence in which things should happen. it is not shaped by the precise timing in which you do or do not achieve something. it's a beautiful kind of chaos made easier when you embrace the lessons fully with a warm hug and patience.

Enjoy Velvet Dragonflies *as an audiobook,*
wherever audiobooks are sold.

Andrews McMeel Publishing
a division of Andrews McMeel Universal
1130 Walnut Street, Kansas City, Missouri 64106

www.andrewsmcmeel.com

22 23 24 25 26 RR2 10 9 8 7 6 5 4 3 2 1

ISBN: 978-1-5248-7680-7

Library of Congress Control Number: 2022939468

Editor: Patty Rice
Art Director/Designer: Diane Marsh
Production Editor: Meg Daniels
Production Manager: Julie Skalla

ATTENTION: SCHOOLS AND BUSINESSES